Shoebills

by Grace Hansen

Abdo Kids Jumbo is an Imprint of Abdo Kids
abdobooks.com

abdobooks.com

Published by Abdo Kids, a division of ABDO, P.O. Box 398166, Minneapolis, Minnesota 55439.
Copyright © 2021 by Abdo Consulting Group, Inc. International copyrights reserved in all countries.
No part of this book may be reproduced in any form without written permission from the publisher.
Abdo Kids Jumbo™ is a trademark and logo of Abdo Kids.

Printed in the United States of America, North Mankato, Minnesota.

052020

092020

 THIS BOOK CONTAINS
RECYCLED MATERIALS

Photo Credits: Alamy, iStock, Minden Pictures, Shutterstock

Production Contributors: Teddy Borth, Jennie Forsberg, Grace Hansen
Design Contributors: Dorothy Toth, Pakou Moua

Library of Congress Control Number: 2019956556
Publisher's Cataloging-in-Publication Data

Names: Hansen, Grace, author.

Title: Shoebills / by Grace Hansen

Description: Minneapolis, Minnesota : Abdo Kids, 2021 | Series: Spooky animals | Includes online resources
    and index.

Identifiers: ISBN 9781098202545 (lib. bdg.) | SBN 9781098203528 (ebook) | ISBN 9781098204013 (Read-
    to-Me ebook)

Subjects: LCSH: Shoebill--Juvenile literature. | Storks--Juvenile literature. | Birds--Behavior--Juvenile
    literature. | Curiosities and wonders--Juvenile literature.

Classification: DDC 596.018--dc23

Table of Contents

Shoebills

Shoebills are large wading birds. They live in swamps and wetlands in Central and Eastern Africa.

Shoebills are nearly 4 feet (1.2 m) tall. Two long legs hold up their **sturdy** bodies.

They are covered in beautiful

blueish-gray feathers.

9

A shoebill's **wingspan** is 8 feet (2.4 m) long! However, flights are rare and short.

Shoebills have big heads. Their
eyes are also remarkably large.

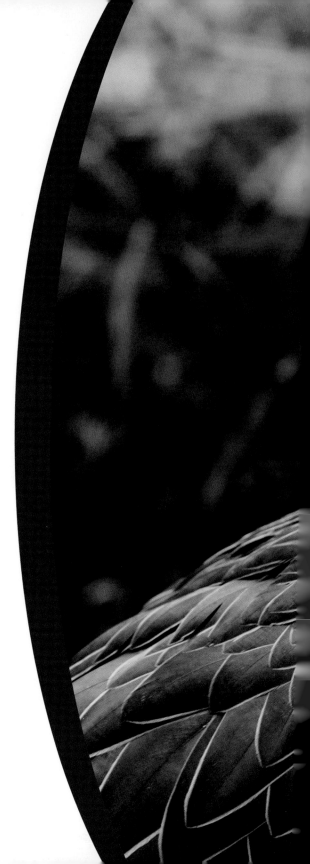

The most notable feature of a shoebill is its giant beak. Its beak ends in a hook and is perfect for catching prey.

Hunting & Food

Shoebills sit and wait for prey. Once they spot prey, they move quickly. They plunge their heads into the water.

17

Shoebills shake their heads from side to side. This helps flick away any plants that they accidentally grabbed. Then they swallow their **prey** whole.

Baby Shoebills

Females lay 1 to 3 eggs at a time. After around 30 days the eggs hatch. Parents feed the chicks until they are big and strong.

More Facts

- Even though shoebills lay a few eggs, just one chick usually survives.

- A shoebill's bill is nearly as wide as it is long.

- The shoebill's scientific name is *balaeniceps rex*, which means "whale-head king."

Glossary

prey – an animal being hunted by another animal for food.

sturdy – strong, hardy, or solid.

wading bird – any type of long-legged birds that wade, or walk slowly with effort, through water in search of food.

wingspan – the distance from the tip of one wing of a bird to the tip of the other wing.

Index

Abdo Kids
ONLINE
FREE! ONLINE MULTIMEDIA RESOURCES

Visit **abdokids.com**
to access crafts, games,
videos, and more!

Use Abdo Kids code

SSK2545

or scan this QR code!